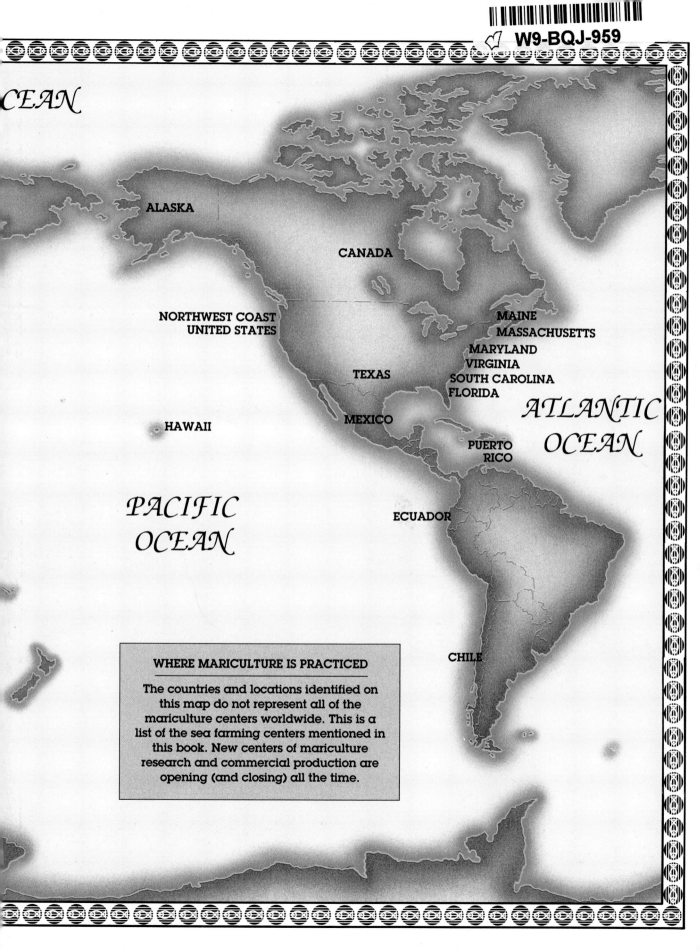

CEAN

ALASKA

CANADA

NORTHWEST COAST
UNITED STATES

MAINE
MASSACHUSETTS
MARYLAND
VIRGINIA
SOUTH CAROLINA
FLORIDA

TEXAS

ATLANTIC
OCEAN

MEXICO

HAWAII

PUERTO
RICO

PACIFIC
OCEAN

ECUADOR

CHILE

WHERE MARICULTURE IS PRACTICED

The countries and locations identified on this map do not represent all of the mariculture centers worldwide. This is a list of the sea farming centers mentioned in this book. New centers of mariculture research and commercial production are opening (and closing) all the time.

MARICULTURE

≈≈≈≈≈≈≈≈≈≈≈≈≈≈≈≈≈≈≈≈≈≈≈≈≈≈

Farming the Fruits
of the Sea

Frances King Koch

FRANKLIN WATTS
New York ● London ● Toronto ● Sydney
A New England Aquarium Book

ACKNOWLEDGMENTS

The author thanks the following people for their great patience and invaluable help in the development of this book: Peter Moore, former director of the Maine Aquaculture Innovation Center; Sam Chapman, aquaculture specialist at the Darling Marine Center, University of Maine; Mike Syslo, of the Massachusetts State Lobster Hatchery; John Corbin, manager of the aquaculture development program at the University of Hawaii; John Ryther, scientist emeritus of Woods Hole Oceanographic Institute; Hank Parker, director of the Northeast Aquaculture Center; and Seth Garfield, oyster farmer and island entrepreneur, Cuttyhunk Island, Massachusetts. Particular thanks are owed to Manisha Gambhir of the New England Aquarium for her research assistance. To my family, for their devoted indulgence, I owe thanks beyond words.

The New England Aquarium would also like to thank photographer Robert Ketchum for his contributions to the book, and the Tatsukichi restaurant in Boston for photographs of their sushi bar.

Frontispiece: Mussels and other sea organisms—shrimp, oysters, finfishes and seaweeds—are promising crops for sea farmers.

Photographs copyright ©: Thomas C. Boyden: pp. 1, 15, 25 right, 35, 44; The New England Aquarium: pp. 4, 38, 39, 46 (all Kenneth Mallory), 50 (Richard Duggan); Robert Glenn Ketchum: pp. 6, 7, 8, 16, 17, 27, 37, 42, 45, 48; Aquaculture Development Program: p. 9, 13, 19, 20 bottom, 32; North Wind Picture Archives: p. 10; Animals Animals/Earth Scenes: pp. 12, 29 (both Marty Stouffer Productions, Ltd.), 14, 25 bottom left, 34 (all E.R. Degginger), 20 top, 24 bottom, 25 top left (all Zig Leszczynski), 24 top & center, 30 (all G.I. Bernard/OSF), 26 (Colin Milkins/OSF), 40 (Breck P. Kent), 41 (Mike & Elvan Habicht), 49 (Ted Levin); David Cavagnaro: p. 21; Joe Devenney: p. 23; Roger Hanlon: p. 51.

CONTENTS

Introduction
5

Chapter One
MARICULTURE THEN AND NOW
7

Chapter Two
THE FRUITS OF THE SEA
17

Chapter Three
TODAY'S SEA FARM
35

Chapter Four
MARICULTURE'S PROBLEMS AND POTENTIAL
45

Chapter Five
THE SCIENCE OF MARICULTURE
Looking into the Future
49

Glossary
53

Source Notes
54

For Further Reading
55

Index
56

INTRODUCTION

A bright June sun sparkles across the Atlantic Ocean. A tanned, hatless farmer in rubber hip boots hauls another heavy lantern net into his boat as it rocks gently near a small island just off the coast of Massachusetts. Sectioned in three tiers and 3 or 4 feet (0.9–1.2 m) tall, the net resembles a large, wet Chinese lantern. In it are 70 pounds (32 kg) of healthy American oysters. The man quickly sorts the oysters by size. He then fills three bushel bags with tightly closed, cup-shaped oysters, called "keepers,"—each 3 or 4 inches (7.6 or 10.2 cm) long. Most of the remaining 100 oysters he returns to the net, which he throws back into the sea. The bulging bushel bags are then labeled "Cuttyhunk Shellfish Farms" and will be delivered the following day to the kitchen of a Manhattan seafood restaurant.

If you've sampled a freshly opened oyster or a fat pink shrimp lately, chances are good that you've eaten a creature that grew up on a sea farm somewhere in the world. It may have been cage-reared in a lantern net off the coast of New England, or it may have been cultured in a carefully monitored cement "pond" on a modern sea farm in Japan.

But why would farmers grow oysters and shrimps when nature has always done a perfectly good job of it? Who are these sea farmers, and where are their ocean farms? What does "sea farming" mean, and why is it important?

Sea farmers hatch and raise living things that come from the ocean. They do this for three good reasons: (1) Mariculture, the ancient art and modern science of ocean farming, holds tremendous potential for producing food for an increasingly populated and hungry world, (2) mariculture is an important tool for helping to protect and restock valuable ocean animals, and (3) as a relatively new area of scientific exploration, mariculture provides valuable information about the creatures that live in our oceans.

MARICULTURE THEN AND NOW

Mariculture is the offspring of aquaculture, the cultivation of aquatic plants and animals, in either fresh or salt water. The word "aquaculture" comes from the Latin *aqua* for water and "culture," meaning to grow or cultivate. Substituting "mari" for "aqua" simply makes the definition specific to salt water. The focus of this book is on mariculture, the practice of farming the plants and animals of the sea.

How did aquaculture begin? Scientists and historians think it followed closely after the appearance of agriculture, or land-

Left: Seaweeds from farms such as this one in Japan may be eaten in fresh, dried, and liquified forms. Seaweeds also become components of such everyday products as soaps, paints, car polishes, and toothpaste.

Below: Sea farmers in India examine coconut-fiber tiles used to collect baby mussels called "spat," and baby lobsters (a different species from the American lobster). Mussels will grow to marketable size in eight months. Lobster larvae are transferred to growing tubs and tanks on land.

**These large nets suspended above the water from large wooden poles are
one of the many devices fishermen use to collect the fish they farm. They
are called Chinese dip nets and are shown in the waters off Kerala, India.**

based farming. About 10,000 years ago, human beings discovered
that instead of wandering from place to place to find food, they
could stay in one place and grow their own. Raising plants and
animals—respectively called "agriculture" and "animal husbandry"—reduced the time and energy it took to find food, allowing
people time to pursue the study of astronomy, architecture, philoso-
phy, science, mathematics, and politics. Agriculture was one of our
first important steps on the road to civilization.

It's difficult to pinpoint when people learned to cultivate sea
animals and plants. Perhaps the earliest moneymaking aquaculturist on record was a Roman named Sergius Orata. One Roman
historian wrote in the first century A.D. that Sergius Orata cultivated
oysters, not for his own dining pleasure, but in order to "make a
large income."[1]

Several early civilizations practiced fresh- and saltwater aquaculture. Ancient records show that the Japanese raised oysters as
early as 2000 B.C.[2] In China, shellfish farming was already well
under way by 500 B.C. By 100 B.C., the Romans had became pro-
ficient and prolific cultivators of oysters. Fishes with fins were
probably first farmed around 1400 A.D., in Indonesia, where young
milkfish were trapped in coastal ponds at high tide.[3]

By the 1600s, oyster farming was so well-established in England

and France that oysters were considered food for poor people![4] Americans took up oyster cultivation in the middle 1800s, when the oyster populations along the shores of New England and New York were being depleted by overzealous harvesters.[5]

MARICULTURE IN THE UNITED STATES

During the 1700s and 1800s a great many Americans were land farmers, so the science and technology of agriculture grew rapidly along with the rest of the young country. Americans were also developing a booming capture-fishing industry, but sea farming played no role in it. To a large extent, that is still the case today in the United States.

By contrast, in Southeast Asia aquaculture has been part of everyday life for hundreds of years. Fish and shellfish have been traditional sources of animal protein for the people of China, Japan, Indonesia, Thailand, and other countries. But until recently, sea farming was a matter of subsistence—that is, fish were raised mostly to keep food on the family table. Sea farming was not the big business it is in Asia today.

Hawaii's Aquaculture Development Program uses outdoor shrimp ponds such as these to grow shrimp to marketable size. Shrimp have proven to be a worldwide sea farming success.

The drawing shows an oyster farm in France during the 1880s. In the same period, Americans in New York and New England were developing oyster farms to make up for overharvesting.

Americans experimented with aquaculture and fish hatcheries during the late 1800s and early 1900s, in an effort to increase declining wild salmon stocks for sport fishing. But it was not until the 1970s that people began to see that overfishing and pollution were taking a heavy toll on ocean animals. Scientists warned also of the possibility of reaching the "maximum sustainable yield" of the oceans—that is, the limit of what the oceans could provide before some animals would decline in numbers, perhaps to extinction.[6]

Mariculturists, working in the public interest, began reviving fish and shellfish hatcheries in an effort to replenish declining stocks. And private-interest mariculturists were lured by the potential profits in restocking such higher-priced, higher-demand species as oysters, lobsters, and shrimp. Today, American mariculture is still struggling to find both the public and the private support it needs to become a viable industry.

MARICULTURE VERSUS AGRICULTURE

By the year 2025, the world's population is expected to reach eight and a half billion people.[7] And that figure may *double* by the end of the twenty-first century.[8] As our numbers grow, so will our need for food. But now traditional capture fishing has some serious, nontraditional problems. More and bigger fishing fleets are going after fewer fishes, farther away from home ports. The fuel costs of the big fishing fleets are passed along to consumers. Increasingly complex laws regulate who can fish and where. There is also the threat of increased ocean pollution from chemical and municipal wastes and oil spills.

Today more than 95 percent of the world's food supply comes from land plants and animals.[9] Although primitive forms of sea farming have been practiced for centuries in some countries, mariculture as a modern food-growing enterprise lags centuries behind agriculture. In his book *The Sea Against Hunger* marine biologist C.P. Idyll points out that in 1975 sea farmers produced one million tons of farmed sea plants and five million tons of farmed sea animals. Land farmers produced 2.6 *billion* tons of land plants, 115 million tons of animals, plus 447 million tons of milk and eggs![10]

Why hasn't mariculture experienced the same growth that agriculture has? The disparity is especially surprising since our planet is fully two-thirds water! One reason is that we're land animals ourselves, and so we've put more effort into cultivating the fruits of our fields, flocks, and trees rather than the bounty of our seas. We've only just begun looking at the world's oceans as big, blue, fertile fields.

NEW DEMANDS FOR FISH

In the United States and other affluent Western countries, there is growing interest in fish and other seafood. In addition to the considerable evidence that they contain less fat and fewer calories

MARICULTURE
AND AGRICULTURE
THE TIES THAT BIND

"A rice paddy farmer floods his paddies when the tides are high and the monsoon swells rivers, lakes, and reservoirs. The tidal water, entering through simple wooden sluice gates, carries young prawns from the sea, and mullet, pearlspot, and milkfish. They thrive on algal growth and the decomposing rice stalks, which provide shelter as well as food. After three months the sluices are opened again, and fish and prawns are caught in nets attached to the sluice gates—as much as 350 kilos of fish per acre (½ hectare) of paddy field. A simple operation that requires neither much effort nor much money. The fish and prawns fetch a price six times higher than the rice."[1]

—Elisabeth Mann Borgese, *Seafarm*

Photographs of land farming—agriculture—in Colorado, and sea farming—mariculture—in Hawaii, show two ways human beings have learned to grow crops nature alone once provided. Despite the promise of both kinds of farming, the development of mariculture lags far behind that of agriculture.

Mariculture and agriculture are linked. In each, human beings have learned to cultivate the things that nature alone once provided. Other ties also bind mariculture and agriculture today, some involving ways in which people have learned to grow crops that benefit each other.

Seaweeds are one example. People have collected or grown seaweeds to eat for centuries. And they've discovered how to use them to help other things grow. In Asian countries, seaweeds are chopped up and used to fertilize coconut palms. In England, experiments have shown that seaweed fertilizer increases wheat, grass, celery, and apple crops. In Ireland, seaweeds are mixed with sand to make soil in which many vegetables thrive.[2]

The combined farming of aquatic and land organisms—called integrated farming—is another link between agriculture and mariculture. Rice paddy farmers practice a kind of integrated farming in which they harvest both rice, the land-based crop, and fish, the water-based crop.

In the Philippines, experiments showed that farmers who added pig, duck, and chicken manures to their fish ponds would get faster-growing fish and more of them.[3]

There are marine authors and scientists who believe that saltwater aquaculture is simply a subcategory of agriculture. Others see mariculture as a distinct industry. To some extent, the future of American mariculture may rest on the outcome of this debate.

Above: Experiments in England have shown that seaweed fertilizers
can increase production of wheat fields such as these.
There are important links between land and sea farming that
can improve production of both.

Right: Among the ocean animals displayed here at a Seattle marketplace
are salmon and clams, both of which can be farm-cultured.

than red meat, people are attracted to the taste of these foods—
especially the so-called luxury seafood, such as shrimp, lobster,
oysters, and clams.

The domestic fishing industry cannot meet the American demand for fish. In 1990, the United States imported a staggering three
billion pounds (1.4 billion kg), of fish and shellfish, both farmed and
wild-caught, from other countries.[11] The fishing industries of the
countries we import from already face problems similar to those of
our own capture-fishing industry. But many of these countries back
up their commercial fishing fleets with well established fish-farming
industries. Indeed, in view of the problems of the capture-fishing
industry and the increasing pressure on our oceans, it makes good
sense to meet nature more than halfway and cultivate some of
what we've been catching. As captured fish decline, farmed fish
can increase.

C H A P T E R   T W O

THE FRUITS OF
THE SEA

The fruits of the sea are the thousands of ocean-dwelling organisms that benefit people. Farming and ranching them enhances their numbers, consistency of quality, and availability in ways that nature cannot.

Species that are suited to sea farming fall into three groups:

1. Invertebrates (animals without backbones), including crustaceans (shrimp, lobsters) and mollusks (oysters, clams, mussels).

Left: Sales of shrimp, such as these harvested on a farm on the island of Oahu, Hawaii, will probably continue to increase faster than sales of any other food from the sea over the next ten years.

Below: Although the United States plays a small role in shrimp farming, the rest of the world has found it a profitable crop. In 1989, shrimp farmers such as these in Thailand produced 1.2 billion pounds of live shrimp.

2. Finfishes, including salmon, tuna, and a variety of other finny creatures.

3. Seaweeds, including red and brown algae that serve as ingredients in thousands of products ranging from ice cream to lawn fertilizer.

What makes an animal or plant suitable for sea farming? Perhaps the first factor is the market. Farmers who make a business of cultivating sea plants and animals grow what consumers and industries want and will buy: this is "the market."

Shrimp are a good example of a suitable crop. Americans, Japanese, and Europeans have large appetites for shrimp. In 1990, Americans bought $1.8 billion worth of shrimp from China, Ecuador, and Southeast Asia.[1] The United States itself has a domestic wild-caught shrimp industry, and there is some modest, mostly experimental, farming of shrimp as well. This does not, however, meet the domestic demand, a demand that shrimp farmers in shrimp-exporting countries are eager to satisfy.

How a plant or animal is faring in its natural habitat is another factor which can make a species suitable for mariculture. Are its numbers in decline in the wild? Is it in demand? Is it worth the work? Salmon are an example of a species that meets these conditions. Through mariculture, they are once again thriving in many countries.

WHAT MAKES A GOOD SEA CROP?

To be ideal for mariculture, a sea creature should be hardy and resistant to disease. It should reproduce, or at least survive from egg stage, in captivity. It should be numerous, fast-growing, largely inactive, and easy and cheap to feed. Most sea animals don't completely fit these descriptions. Mariculture thus becomes the science of controlling and manipulating certain characteristics of the sea creature to suit the sea farmer's purposes.

To control, change, or improve a plant or animal, sea farmers must first know how and where it lives, how it reproduces, what it eats, what water temperatures it likes, what diseases it gets, and what its predators are. This information and more is collected through the study of life cycles. By observing life cycles, scientists can learn to change them. And sea farmers can use the life-cycle information to develop their crops: fatter, tastier oysters; bigger, faster-growing shrimp; a better survival rate for salmon.

Left: Nearly half the United States supply of farmed shrimp comes from Hawaii. Here a greenhouse-style ceiling helps maintain high temperatures for a shrimp grow-out pool. Right: In the earliest stages of its life cycle, shrimp larvae feed on phytoplankton such as the kinds shown here cultured in glass jars.

CRUSTACEANS

Behold two crustaceans, the lobster and the shrimp: they wear their shell-skeletons on the outside, protecting soft inner bodies. Strange as it seems, they are more closely related to insects than to other sea animals (both are arthropods, or joint-footed creatures). They are always in great demand and may be the most popular edible sea animals on the planet.

SHRIMP

Shrimp have proved a major sea-farming success. They're in enormous demand, they grow quickly, and they're being successfully farmed and exported by several countries. The Japanese were the first to set up a commercial shrimp hatchery in 1959.[2]

The shrimp is a nocturnal sea animal: it buries itself during the day, leaving just eyes and feelers above the mud, and comes out at night to hunt for food. Catching wild shrimp usually entails trawling—dragging nets over the sea bottom.

LOBSTERS
EXPENSIVE, FEROCIOUS, AND FUSSY

It's expensive to raise a lobster.

That is probably why nobody farms them commercially yet. It's not that we don't know how.

Homarus americanus—the scientific name for the American lobster, the Maine kind—can and will breed in captivity. But the best supplies of lobster eggs come from wild-caught "berried" lobsters. Berried lobsters are females with 5,000 to 125,000 tiny berry-shaped eggs attached to their undersides. The eggs hatch easily in the mariculturist's tank. Then things get difficult.

From the moment they hatch, lobsters are cannibals, so they can't be raised in groups. Keeping them in separate apartments is pricey, though one adventurous lobster farmer is trying this. They're slow growers, too, in their native habitats; a New England lobster farmer won't get a mature, marketable crop for five to eight years. They are also fussy eaters; only fresh food will do. Lobster babies in hatcheries are fed ground beef liver or clams, and mashed brine shrimp. Adults prefer fresh fish or shellfish. Artificial foods have been tried, but are prohibitively expensive.

Lobsters can be raised in tanks successfully. Researchers at the Massachusetts State Lobster Hatchery on Martha's Vineyard kept a live lobster in a tank for ten years. This is still a far cry from nature's record; in the wild, lobsters can live from 50 to 100 years!

Large-clawed lobsters such the one above are shipped to customers all over the world. If sea farmers can overcome such problems as lobster cannibalism, and fussy eating habits, lobster mariculture may become a booming business. By isolating individual lobsters as they grow, this sea farmer in Hawaii's aquaculture program prevents the lobsters from eating one another.

Aerial views of Laguna de Bay, in the Philippines, show how fish traps, probably for milkfish, are arranged to catch fish which come in with the rising tides. Once the fish are in the pens, the entrance is blocked and they can't swim out again.

There are no major commercial shrimp farms in the United States. Still, sea farmers hope that experimental shrimp operations now under way in Puerto Rico, Texas, South Carolina, and Hawaii will eventually become commercially productive. The American farmed shrimp that do appear on the market amount to only two million pounds (900,000 kg)—a fraction of what Americans eat— and nearly half of that is produced in Hawaii. Elsewhere in the world, shrimp farmers produced a record crop in 1990: 663,000 metric tons (732,600,000 pounds), or roughly 25 percent of all shrimp on the market. Just ten years ago, farmers were producing only two percent of the world's shrimp.[3] Americans continue to depend on large shrimp imports from China, Ecuador, Mexico, and Southeast Asia.[4]

SHRIMP LIFE ON THE FARM

Some commercial shrimp farmers in Asia still culture shrimp the old way, by raising the tiny animals brought into their ponds by the tides or buying newly spawned eggs from vendors. Today most species of shrimp can be raised entirely in captivity, so farmers can control all phases of the shrimp life cycle.

The eggs hatch within 13 or 14 hours of spawning. The nauplius, as each shrimp baby is called, feeds on its own yolk sac for a day and a half. Then, as a zoea, it is ready for a diet of tiny sea plants and animals called diatoms and zooplankton. About four days and several molts later, it emerges as a mysis, with a tail similar to its mother's and an appetite for ground oyster or clam eggs and brine shrimp.[5] There are several more molts, and about ten days after hatching, the baby becomes a postlarva feeding on minced tuna and tiny brine shrimp. Now it looks like a miniature shrimp and is either shipped out to other farms for rearing or put into rearing ponds by the farmer.[6] By the time a shrimp reaches adulthood, it can eat an artificial pellet-like food made from fish and shrimp meal.[7]

Shrimp sales probably will continue to increase faster than sales of any other seafood in the next decade. In 1989, shrimp farmers produced 1.2 billion pounds (½ billion kg) of live shrimp.[8] The

Life Cycle of a Prawn (A Large Shrimp)

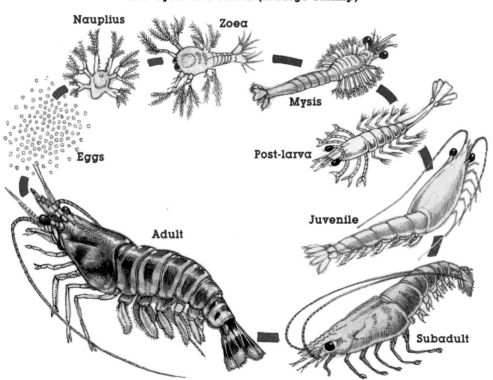

One problem with farming lobsters is not knowing what happens to the young farm-grown lobsters after they're released from the hatchery into the ocean. Scientists have no reliable way to track them. Tagging the youngsters' shells doesn't work because growing lobsters molt often.

In Maine, lobster mariculturists are experimenting with shell color as a tagging method. Starting with the eggs of a rare blue-shelled "egger" named Amanda (an egger is a lobster that bears eggs, and this egger's shell really is a distinct blue), mariculturist Sam Chapman and his colleagues at the Darling Marine Center at the University of Maine released 5,800 blue penny-sized lobster babies into the Atlantic Ocean in 1988. Divers found evidence that some survived, but Chapman says it's too early to tell how many will reach adulthood. He hopes to keep track of Amanda's blue babies (most American lobsters have reddish-orange or greenish shells) and learn about the survival rates of hatchery-raised lobsters.

Blue lobsters are natural genetic variations on the usual reddish-orange and reddish-green lobsters. When they are cultivated in the laboratory and released to the wild, they may help researchers studying lobsters' survival rates.

United States did not play much of a role in that production, nor is it likely to soon. American shrimp farming is limited by economics: land and labor costs are too high, and coastal regulations too restrictive, for the industry to be profitable. Ecuador, a leader in farmed shrimp, has 1,500 shrimp farms, 75 packing plants, and 80 hatcheries.[9] American shrimp farmers know they must compete with imported shrimp produced at a much lower cost.

MOLLUSKS

Mollusks, or bivalves, are sea animals that live in the space formed by two hinged shells. They are among our oldest seafood. Sea

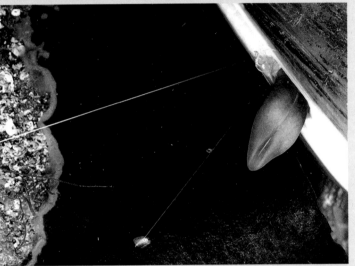

Above: The mussel attaches itself to underwater surfaces by a network of sticky hairs called byssus. It uses its strong foot to tear the hairs so it can move from one location to another. Below: Filter-feeding animals such as mussels absorb chemicals from the water. The controlled conditions of a sea farm help ensure that they can be marketed.

DEVELOPING A GOOD SET OF MUSSELS

A mussel may release up to 15 million eggs at a time.[1] Within four hours of spawning, the eggs become larvae, called veligers. They swim and float along on water currents for about two weeks,[2] then attach themselves to rocks, plants, old shells, and other surfaces. It's at this point that mussel farmers collect them.[3]

Mussels develop a strong muscular foot and a tuft of tough sticky hairs, called byssus, by which they secure themselves to their ocean homes. If you've ever seen a mussel being prepared for cooking, you know these tough hairs, the mussel's "beard," must be removed.

The mussel eats just as oysters do, by filtering seawater rich in plankton through its siphons and gills. Its growth depends on several things: the flow of the water currents—the faster the better since more food comes along in fast-flowing water; the amount of light—the less the better; and the temperature of the water—it takes longer to grow in cold water than warm.[4] Mussels grow in profusion and often compete for space with oysters in some American waters.

Most mussel farmers today are in France, Holland, and Spain. By far the leader in mussel production, Spain produces 500,000 tons a year.[5]

Mussels are not in as great demand as other bivalves in the United States. But as our healthy diet concerns grow, we may turn increasingly to this little package of nutritious low-fat, low-calorie health food.

Soft-Shell Clam

Dungeness Crab

Giant Rock Scallop

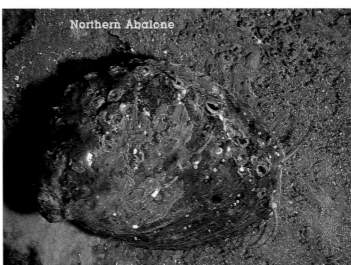
Northern Abalone

All these invertebrate animals have potential for mariculture, although not all have been successful. Crabs, like lobsters, have to be isolated to survive and this makes their farming costly. Abalone, scallop, and soft-shell clam farmers don't have to be concerned with cannibalism because these animals are filter feeders and don't eat each other.

farmers today grow a variety of these shell dwellers, including oysters, clams, scallops, and mussels. Traditionally, the most popular has been the oyster.

OYSTERS

"Secret, and self-contained, and solitary as an oyster," wrote Charles Dickens to describe Old Marley in *A Christmas Carol*. There is a mystique about oysters—their ancient history, rich store of legends; the devotion paid them and their place of distinction in today's popular "raw" bars.

But looking at today's oyster farms, it's hard to think of oysters as being solitary or secret. They are grown in such enormous quantities that by the year 2000, the annual production could reach 2 million metric tons.[10]

Oysters are the closest of any animal to being perfect sea-farm crops. The oyster farmer can control nearly every phase of their lives, from spawn to harvest. Commercially, they are nearly ideal: there is always a great demand, they grow quickly, are easy to feed, and they don't travel. Although they grow in profusion in the wild, pollution, overfishing, and predators have reduced natural stocks. Because they are laboriously tended, farmed oysters are larger, often better-tasting, and usually more expensive than wild oysters.[11]

AN OYSTER'S FARM LIFE

A single oyster can spawn as many as 100 million eggs at one time.[12] In the natural habitat, a large number of offspring will not survive because of disease, predators, storms, and lack of food.[13] In oyster hatcheries, survival rates are better because of meticulous tending. Some oyster farmers specialize in this nursery phase, hatchery-rearing tiny "seed" oysters which they sell to other farmers to grow to market size.

Oysters spawn when the water temperature reaches a certain level. In nature, this generally occurs as ocean waters warm up in the spring. Modern oyster farmers, working in controlled conditions, can dictate when spawning will take place. They increase the water temperature slowly to just above 83 degrees F (28°C) and the

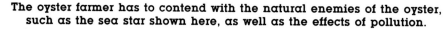

The oyster farmer has to contend with the natural enemies of the oyster, such as the sea star shown here, as well as the effects of pollution.

In Ise Bay, Japan, rafts made of cedar logs or bamboo poles serve as rearing cages for young oysters.

tank-dwelling oysters begin releasing eggs and sperm into the water.[14]

The tiny fragile larvae—each measures about $\frac{1}{75}$ of an inch ($\frac{1}{3}$ mm) in length—that develop from the eggs swim around for about two weeks and then, at the stage at which they are known as "spat," attach themselves to any firm, clean surface. Oyster farmers in different countries use various surfaces for collecting their spat. In France, coated roofing tiles[15] are popular; in parts of Japan, bamboo and wire lines are used; in the Philippines, tin cans are attached to bamboo poles. Elsewhere, old oyster shells, called "cultch," are laid down on the sea floor. In many landside oyster hatcheries, the spat settle in tanks on bushels of oyster shells.

When oysters reach fingernail size, in four to six weeks, they are planted in prepared beds in tidal flats or shallow bays. There, they feed on phytoplankton (tiny marine plants) brought in by the tides. Tending them means thinning out the shell clusters and ridding them of starfish or other predators. Oysters take two to five years to become adults, depending on water temperatures and other conditions. In off-bottom oyster cultures, the animals live in nets suspended in the water, never touching bottom.

Oysters are farmed in many countries—the Netherlands, England, Canada, and the United States. In Japan, a major industry is devoted to producing baby "seed" oysters that are exported to the United States and Canada or sold to other Japanese oyster farmers.[16] France is the major producer of the flat-shell oyster served as the raw "oyster on the halfshell."[17]

Wild oysters were harvested along the east coast of the United States starting in the 1600s, and oyster farming has gone on there and in the Gulf coast region since the late 1800s.[18] In the last 30 years, many Atlantic coast oyster beds have been wiped out by disease, overfishing, bad weather, and poor water quality. Most large oystering businesses now operate along the Pacific Ocean coast, although smaller companies and seed hatcheries are still active on the East Coast.[19]

Mariculturists in Florida, South Carolina, and Virginia are beginning to farm hard clams—little necks, cherrystones, or quahogs[20]—in addition to oysters. One adventuresome farmer in Buzzards Bay, Massachusetts, operates what may be the first commercial scallop farm in the country.[21] Bay scallops were plentiful in Buzzards Bay until overfishing and pollution wiped out most natural stocks.

FINFISH

In some parts of the world finfish culture is as old as oyster culture. The Chinese began to cultivate carp in ponds more than one thousand years ago. Today, a large number of freshwater finfish are farmed throughout the world, including trout, catfish (especially successful in the United States), pike, perch, bass, smelt, and a range of other species. Of the saltwater finfish farmed today, salmon may be mariculture's greatest success story.

SALMON

Salmon once thrived in American and Canadian waters. But by the early 1900s, their numbers were dangerously low due to overfishing, dam building, logging and other constructions. Since the 1970s, salmon have begun to thrive again along the Pacific and Atlantic coasts, thanks to the efforts of mariculturists.

Salmon return from the ocean to the river of their birth to lay their eggs. One way of raising salmon, called ranching, is to let the eggs develop and hatch in a sea farm and then release them to the wild a year later. When the matured salmon return years later to spawn, they can be harvested.

Salmon is both farmed and ranched today. In ranching, the salmon are hatched from eggs spawned and fertilized in the hatchery and raised to the "smolt" stage, when they're about a year old and roughly the size of an adult's finger. Then they're released to make their way to the ocean, where they may live for two to five years before they are caught by fishermen or they return to their hatcheries to spawn. Salmon are anadromous fish, meaning that they always attempt to return to their freshwater birthplaces to spawn.

Farmed salmon don't make the journey from the hatchery to the sea and back, as ranched fish do, nor do they find their own food. At smolt size, they are put into large open-ocean cages where they live until harvest time. The cages are actually huge net pens suspended from floating buoys, where the salmon are hand- or machine-fed, cared for, and protected from predators. Occasionally they're sorted by size and moved to different cages. In

Life Cycle of the Sockeye Salmon

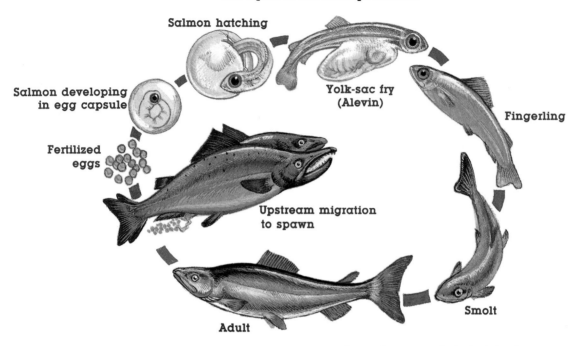

Salmon hatching

Salmon developing in egg capsule

Yolk-sac fry (Alevin)

Fingerling

Fertilized eggs

Upstream migration to spawn

Adult

Smolt

Inside the transparent eggs below lie tiny salmon ready to hatch. One has already escaped its egg capsule, but still depends on an attached yolk sac for nourishment.

about 18 months, when they are between 8 and 12 pounds (3.6 to 5.4 kg) and about two and a half years old, they're harvested.

Several countries are engaged in salmon farming, including Norway, Scotland, Ireland, Japan, Chile, Canada, and the United States. Norway is the clear leader, producing more than half of all farmed salmon on the world market. Total world production of farmed salmon in 1990 was 277,500 metric tons; of that, Norway produced nearly 160,000 metric tons, while the United States and Canada together contributed 24,825 tons.[22]

Other finfish farmed around the world include yellowtail, the main saltwater finfish farmed in Japan, and red seabream. In and around the Caspian Sea, farms produce the mighty sturgeon, an anadromous fish that yields sturgeon roe, or caviar.[23]

SEAWEEDS

Seaweeds are, literally, plants that grow in seawater. Coastal-dwelling people throughout history have gathered seaweeds by hand, rake, boat, and now by machine. They have put seaweeds to uses as varied as the imagination can devise. Seaweeds are eaten fresh, dried, and liquified. They are grazed upon by land animals, used as fertilizer, and made into bread. They are used to make toothpaste, cloth, paper bags, baby pants, soaps, paints, car polishes, and food wrappers. A full 50 percent of the algae harvested around the world today is used by the chemical industry.[24]

Scientists classify the 15,000 species of seaweeds, or macroalgae, by color and by other characteristics: there are blue-green, brown, and red seaweeds. The brown and red varieties are the most valuable commercially.[25]

Do we eat seaweeds today? Absolutely, although they are mostly in forms we don't recognize as seaweed. Processed, they become thickeners in low-fat milk, gelatin desserts, baby formula, chocolate syrup, and instant breakfast drinks. We wear them too, as in cosmetics; and we construct and decorate buildings with them, in paper, paint, and rubber that contain seaweed extracts.

While natural kelp is harvested along the California coast and there is some experimental kelp farming in Hawaii, Americans do not farm seaweeds commercially. Seaweeds are widely farmed only in Japan, China, and the Pacific Islands.[26]

In Japan, nori (its scientific name is *Porphyra*) is an important, extensively farmed ocean product. Nori is a popular condiment for

Hawaii's Aquaculture Development Program uses indoor greenhouses and nets suspended in the water as grow-out areas for the seaweed called nori. Nori can be cut and dried, then crisped and crushed to make flavoring for soups and sauces.

the Japanese dining table. You may know nori as the delicate wrapping around the popular Japanese food known as sushi (raw fish). Nori is widely farmed in bays, gulfs, and lagoons.[27]

Cultured in Asian waters since the late 1600s,[28] nori is still farmed by some Japanese using the traditional method. Plant spores from the sea are collected on bundles of bamboo branches or other tree twigs pushed into the muddy ocean bottom. The branches are then moved closer to shore, where the plants mature in brackish, nutrient-rich water. In modern nori farming, the spores are artificially produced in laboratories and then cultured on large nets suspended horizontally over the sea's surface. With tidal action, the nets dip into the water and the growing plants are nourished. This method yields a larger and more reliable supply of healthy plants than does the traditional method.[29]

Mature nori plants have large, bright purple leaves, each about 1½ feet (½ m) long. After being harvested, the plants are washed, cut into small pieces and mixed with fresh water, dried on mats in the sun, and marketed as "hoshinori" in large flat sheets. In the Japanese kitchen, it is heated, crisped, crushed, and used to flavor sauces and soups.[30] In the United States nearly $50 million worth of imported nori is consumed a year, and entrepreneurs are attempting to farm it in Maine and the American Northwest.[31] It is also cultivated in China and Taiwan.

The Japanese also farm a second seaweed, *Undaria*, a brown algae they call "wakame." The Chinese are successfully cultivating *Laminaria*, another type of brown algae. And a species of red algae, scientifically known as *Eucheuma*, is farmed in the Philippines.[32]

Research into other uses for seaweeds continues worldwide. Scientists have experimented with using seaweeds for human nutrition and for treating sewage effluent. They have tested strains of algae for use in producing electric power. There is considerable research into the potential use of certain algae in medical research and disease treatment.

As marine science and technology become even more sophisticated, the list of ocean-farmed plants and animals will certainly grow longer.

ON YOUR OWN

- When you see salmon in the fish market, ask the clerk where it came from.

- Salmon farming represents a mariculture success. Research how salmon fishing began and how it led to salmon farming.

- Ever eaten seaweed? Try some sushi at a Japanese restaurant. Sushi and sashimi are small parcels of raw seafood (sushi includes rice, too) usually wrapped in nori.

TODAY'S SEA FARM

A shrimp farm in Indonesia might consist of 50 one- to five-acre (½- to 2-hectare) ponds in which shrimp and other fish are growing. A salmon farm in Norway might be a ship-size cage system in which hundreds of thousands of young salmon are being reared. An oyster farm in New England might include 800,000 oysters on a two-acre lease in a saltwater bay. Each is a sea farm where living things are grown.

SEA FARMING AND SEA RANCHING

There are two ways to cultivate sea animals—through sea farming and sea ranching. They differ in the amount of care that is given the "crop" in each.

Left: Young salmon are reared to harvest size—between 8 and 12 pounds (3.6–5.4 kg)—in open-ocean cages at a salmon nursery in Norway. Norway produces more than half of all farmed salmon on the world market today.

Below: One way to develop salmon as a food is to grow it in open-ocean cages through all of its life stages, until harvest time. This group of juvenile coho salmon can be fed and tended until they become adults.

In sea *farming*, the farmer controls all or nearly all phases of an animal's life, from birth to harvest.[1] The farmer cultivates egg-bearing animals, collects their eggs, fertilizes and hatches them, feeds the young, rears them to adulthood, and sells them. A good example is today's salmon farmer. The farm animals are hatched, fed, and tended from start to finish. And they remain the property of the farmer.

There are some variations. The hatchery farmer specializes in eggs, or "seed" stock, which is sold to other farmers. The grow-out farmer buys the seed stock from a nursery farmer, or collects it from the wild, and raises it to maturity.

In sea *ranching*, the mariculturist typically raises ocean animals in captivity only when they are young, and then releases them to the sea. Once in the sea, they belong to whoever catches them. If they are anadromous fish, like salmon, many will eventually return to the place where they were hatched.

In both sea farming and sea ranching, attempts are made to simulate the natural habitat of the cultured animal.

FARMING WITH RAFTS, LINES, AND NETS

Oysters are traditionally farmed in France and the United States by being tucked into beds in tidal flats or shallow bay bottoms. In some countries, farmers use various forms of off-bottom culturing as well.

In his book *Harvest of the Sea*, marine biologist John Bardach describes a Japanese oyster farm in the Inland Sea near Hiroshima. The typical farmer there uses big bamboo rafts, perhaps 30 by 45 feet (10 by 15 m) each, supported on floating barrels. The farmer may have up to 100 rafts. Attached to each are many lines or wires, strung with clean clamshells, that hang 20 feet (7 m) down into the water. When oysters spawn during July and August, the oyster "spat" collects on the shells and grows in dense masses. As the oysters grow, the rafts sink down with their weight and new supporting barrels may be added. During the season, the farmer often thins out the oysters to allow more growing room.

The advantage in this farming method is that the lines do not touch the bottom and the oysters are thus protected from starfish and bottom silt that may harbor disease-bearing bacteria. Another plus is that the farmer benefits from the depth of the water column, obtaining a far larger and more efficient crop than if only the flat sea bottom were used.[2] At harvest time, in January or February, the oyster lines are hoisted up and emptied.

Mussels such as these seen drying in the sun have yet to attract as much consumer interest in the United States as oysters, clams, and scallops.

Oyster farmer Seth Garfield uses a slightly different off-bottom method. His small grow-out pond on Cuttyhunk Island, off the Massachusetts coast, contains long strings of floating buoys, each of which secures a large suspended lantern net that contains up to 200

Seth Garfield, New England oyster farmer, travels by skiff across the tidal pond where his oysters are being grown out on the Massachusetts island of Cuttyhunk. A string of white buoys stretches across the pond. Each buoy marks a suspended off-bottom lantern net, which contains the growing oysters.

AN OYSTERMAN IN NEW ENGLAND

Seth Garfield is a New England sea farmer. He owns and operates Cuttyhunk Shellfish Farms, specializing in farmed American and French belon oysters. He follows a long tradition of East Coast oystering, one that began in the 1800s.

Oystering in the winter on Cuttyhunk Island is "routine," Garfield says. His 800,000 to a million oysters live in about 800 lantern nets suspended in six feet (2m) of water in a tide-fed pond. A two-person crew is all that's required for the occasional harvesting, cleaning, and weeding of the crop. In water colder than 48 degrees F (9° Celsius), oysters hibernate, don't spawn, and don't grow very much.

But in April the water in the 40-acre (16-hectare) pond begins to change. Nutrient-laden wastes from the oysters fertilize plants growing in and on the pond. The plants cover the pond surface in excess in some areas, keeping the water underneath too warm for the oysters. And seabird droppings contaminate the pond. Massachusetts requires that sea farmers take regular water samples. When these show that the pond water isn't ideal for oyster rearing (that is, when the levels of bacteria from the bird wastes start climbing), Garfield must move his inventory to an open-ocean site. State environmental officials generally close the pond to oyster harvesting in the summer months.

So for several days starting in May, before the pond becomes unhealthy, Garfield and his crew hoist the four-foot- (1⅓-m) long lantern nets—each one holding around 200 oysters—onto a motorized wooden skiff, transfer them to a flatbed truck, and drive them to the town pier. There, they are loaded onto his oyster boat that delivers them to a two-acre (¾-hectare) site in a sheltered bay on nearby Penikese Island.

At Penikese (PEN-a-kees) the nets are dropped over the side, attached to long strings of buoys, and the oysters are allowed to grow out over the summer. Also at Penikese is Garfield's holding "warehouse," a four-sided dock, 24 feet (8 m) per side, with a screened open-bottom well in which he drops and briefly stores bushel bags of harvested oysters.

Harvesting and shipping take place all summer: Garfield runs a wholesale oyster business that serves local restaurants and some as far away as New York City. He also operates Cuttyhunk Harbor's only floating raw bar. Every day, rain or shine, from 4 P.M. to 8 P.M., he and his raw bar crew motor from yacht to yacht in the harbor selling freshly shucked oysters and wild-harvested cherrystone clams. Landlubbers can buy them at the Cuttyhunk Shellfish Farms "corporate world headquarters," as Garfield calls his shack on the town pier.

In the fall, the oysters at Penikese are moved back to winter in the Cuttyhunk pond. Garfield replenishes his oyster stock by purchasing two-inch (5-cm) "seed" oysters from a hatchery on Fishers Island, New York. He calls himself strictly a "grow-out" oyster farmer.

Garfield hauls up and examines a lantern net. Garfield takes several lantern nets ashore and empties them onto a sorting table where he sorts the oysters by size and cleans off plant growth or predators. Then he either sets them aside to sell at market if they are large enough, or returns them to the nets for further growth. Garfield opens an oyster by inserting a sharp shucking knife between the shells and prying them apart. Inside is a perfect marketable oyster, ready to eat on the half-shell!

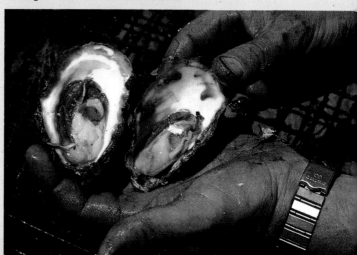

Oyster farming has other rewards in addition to providing a delicious food. Four species of sea oysters are raised to produce pearls.

oysters. The oysters thrive in the nets, are periodically cleaned and thinned, and are kept safe from predators. The nets make harvesting the oysters easier: dredging is required to harvest bottom-planted oysters, and Garfield can cultivate many more animals in suspended cages than he could on the bottom.

In Spain, the largest producer of mussels, raft-and-line culturing is used extensively.[3] In some oyster hatcheries in the United States and elsewhere, farmers spawn and rear oysters in cement tanks on trays and in net bags. Generally, these are later planted in traditional oyster beds on the ocean bottom.

POND CULTURE

For eight centuries, Southeast Asian sea farmers have used tidal ponds to culture edible sea animals, including the milkfish,[4] a popular food fish that looks like a plump herring. Thousands of milkfish ponds, located in tidal flats, still are made by clearing mangrove swamps and diking them with mud or other materials.[5]

40

In a primitive form, pond culture is simple: shrimp or milkfish ride into the ponds on an incoming tide and are kept from riding out again by sluice gates across the pond entrances. There, the animals live on tidal algae until they are mature enough for harvesting. The farmer does little work until harvest time. The pond may yield several different harvestable species, depending upon what the tides have brought in.

In more sophisticated forms of pond farming, especially where milkfish are the main crop, the farmer stocks "nursery" ponds with small fry collected from the wild or purchased from fry vendors. These are reared to fingerling size and then either resold to other farmers to raise or moved to the farmer's own "grow-out" ponds, where they mature within several months.[6] Shrimp are sometimes raised as a secondary crop along with the milkfish.

FISHFACT
FISH FARMING STATISTICS

When statisticians talk about the commercial "landings" of fish, they mean those supplies of aquatic animals that are taken from the water, fresh or salt, for sale on the market. Both aquaculture and commercial fishing contribute yearly to commercial fish landings.

When they measure these landings, statisticians use the term "metric tons." A metric ton (spelled "tonne" in Europe) equals 2,240 pounds, a bit more than the 2,000 pound United States ton. Because of worldwide use of the metric system, statistics are often recorded in metric units.

Among the ocean fishes displayed here at a Seattle marketplace is a species of salmon, more and more of which may be farmed in open-ocean cages rather than being caught in the wild.

In the Philippines and Japan, shrimp for world markets are raised by what is called intensive pond farming. This combines traditional pond culture and modern technology, with the objective of raising the greatest number of shrimp in as little space as possible. Farmers use concrete tanks, artificial foods, and sophisticated water circulation systems to inhibit disease. Instead of using traditional earthen ponds, huge numbers of shrimp are cultured in greenhouse-style nursery tanks and then reared to maturity in outdoor ¼-acre (⅛-hectare) concrete tanks. Typically, a farmer places a berried (egg-bearing) shrimp into a tank where it spawns 500,000 to a million eggs.[7] The farmer immediately removes it from the nursery tank—like the lobster, it is cannibalistic—and cultures the young for about 50 days. They are then moved to outdoor rearing tanks.[8] It takes three to six months to produce market-size shrimp.

The fenced-off corrals in this bay in the Philippines are for farming milkfish, an important food fish. Here baby fishes can be reared to juvenile size or grown to marketable adults.

Cage culture is proving valuable—if controversial—for finfish farmers the world over, particularly those raising salmon. Near-shore cages permit complete control over these fast-moving, muscular fish, from egg to harvest, and provide access to a salmon harvest on demand. That means a buyer of a farmed salmon will probably get a fish that is fresher than one caught in the wild, put into storage on the boat, transported to shore, frozen and finally shipped to market.

In a typical modern salmon cage system, the fish live for about a year and a half in large net enclosures that hang from floating steel or timber grids. Each enclosure, or pen, can contain thousands of young fish. Walkways installed around each pen allow the farmer access to the fish for handling, feeding, and harvesting. Additional nets over the top or around the pens discourage diving and swimming predators, including birds and seals.[9] The grids can form cage systems sometimes as large as ships.[10] For maximum efficiency, the cages are anchored in fast-moving currents that cleanse them of fish waste and uneaten food and protect them from disease.

Nevertheless, to many not in the fish farming business, the cages seem less than ideal. In Scotland, Norway, Canada, and the United States, coastal residents complain that the cages are unsightly; that salmon wastes can foul local waters and threaten natural fish stocks. Carried into courts of law, these objections have prevented some salmon farmers from obtaining the permits they need.

ON YOUR OWN

- If you live near the warm waters of Southern California or the Gulf Coast, imagine you plan to become a shrimp farmer. Ask your state's environmental agencies what regulations and permits you need to start your shrimp farm. Begin with the nearest Sea Grant Program and state environmental agency.

- If you live in New England, or the Pacific Northwest, talk to an oyster farmer. Find out what it would take to begin an oyster farm in your area.

CHAPTER FOUR

MARICULTURE'S PROBLEMS AND POTENTIAL

Mariculture's potential today is tremendous. The science and technology necessary to make sea farming productive are already here, and research into improving many farmed species is well under way. Most scientists agree that mariculture could help ease the problem of world hunger. Commercial companies as well as private entrepreneurs are investing in sea farming experiments. In Asia and parts of Europe, mariculture is already big business.

But there are heavy constraints. In the United States especially, sea farmers face daunting legal, economic, and political challenges. The concept of sea farming is new to Americans. Costs for sea farming labor and land are high. And since most sea farming is

Left: Mounds of thousands upon thousands of shells result from the oyster's popularity as a seafood. But their presence on the seashore, and the problems of disposing of them, conflict with the interests of real estate developers and commercial fishing companies.

Below: Cuttlefish dry in the sun in a village in southern India. This relative of the octopus and the squid is a popular food animal outside the United States.

Restaurant sushi bars offer such delicacies as raw tuna, salmon, rice, and cucumber encased in a wrapping of nori seaweed.

practiced on or near an ocean coast, mariculture must compete with other, more established, coastal activities—such as real estate, commercial fishing, and industrial and manufacturing businesses that require proximity to the ocean. In addition, many environmentalists have protested against sea farming, claiming that sea farmers use feeds and disease-protection chemicals that interfere with natural fish stocks. Also, state and federal laws regulating coastal uses are complex and sometimes confusing. Rigorous permit processes for starting a fish farm have discouraged many would-be farmers on both ocean coasts.

The picture elsewhere, as we've seen, is quite different. Where mariculture is woven into the fabric of a nation's history, culture, and business enterprise, the challenges to sea farming are not often institutional. In Japan, for example, seafood production is a national priority. Ownership of prime coastal locations is already in the hands of those who operate fishing or aquacultural operations and so there are no conflicting use problems. Indeed, in Japan, the challenges are based on environmental issues. With increasingly polluted inshore waters, the Japanese are conducting many of their farming operations farther out at sea.[1]

These constraints aside, mariculture's potential for producing food is as vast as the ocean itself. In 1988, out of 93 million metric tons of fish landings, 14 million were produced through aquaculture. Of that 14 million, 8 million came from sea farms.[2] The United Nations Food and Agricultural Organization predicts ocean farms could produce 22 million tons of sea animals by the year 2000. John Ryther, scientist emeritus of the Woods Hole Oceanographic Institute in Massachusetts, estimates that ocean farming could someday produce 100 million tons of food a year. Marine biologist C.P. Idyll raises the estimate to 125 million tons a year and says that if we sharpen our understanding of the sea and how to manage it, even larger harvests might be possible—perhaps up to 400 million tons.[3]

ON YOUR OWN

- Image you are a senator from a coastal state. Write a policy statement supporting mariculture research and development for your state.
- There are 2,240 pounds in one metric ton. How many pounds of farmed seafood were produced during 1988?
- Pick one of America's coastal states. Find out what industries and businesses are located on that coast. Would that state be a good site for a sea farm? Why or why not?
- Become an aquatic farmer at home—set up an aquarium. Freshwater aquariums are easy and inexpensive to maintain. If you're brave, tackle a saltwater aquarium. Consult your local aquarium store and these books and magazines to get started:

Aquarium Fish, by Joan Palmer. New York: Bookwright, 1989.
Caring for Your Fish, by Mark McPherson. Mahwah, NJ: Troll, 1985.
Freshwater and Marine Aquarium Magazine, Sierra Madre, CA: R/C Modeler Co. Monthly.
The Marine Aquarium Reference—Systems and Invertebrates. Plantation, FL: Green Turtle Publications, 1989. An adult book.
Simon & Schusters' Complete Guide to Freshwater and Marine Aquarium Fishes. New York: Simon & Schuster, 1976. An adult book.
Taking Care of Your Fish, by Joyce Pope. New York: Franklin Watts, 1987.
Tropical Fish Hobbyist Magazine, Neptune City, NJ: TFH Publications Monthly.

THE SCIENCE OF MARICULTURE

LOOKING INTO THE FUTURE

Scientists are working both to improve edible farmed animals and plants through crossbreeding (hybridization) and genetic manipulation, and to find new ones to cultivate for other purposes. Among experiments in fish and shellfish breeding are those aimed at producing hardier, more disease- and pesticide-resistant animals, and those that can survive in temporarily polluted waters.[1]

Important mariculture-related work is taking place in biomedical research centers. One lab in Galveston, Texas, farms squids used by scientists to study human nerve cell functions and diseases affecting the nervous system. The National Cancer Institute in Bethesda, Maryland, tests more than 1,000 sea organisms a year—mostly plants and invertebrates—to determine whether they might

Left: On this farm in Calcutta, India, recycled sewage water is used to fertilize vegetables such as cabbages and eggplant, and then helps feed a population of freshwater fishes that include carp, tilapia, and catfish. Cultivating many kinds of fishes in the same growing area is called polyculture and was first practiced centuries ago in China. Although the scene here is a freshwater farm, polyculture has potential for sea farming as well.

Below: An Atlantic salmon farm in Maine, shows one of the many advantages of growing fish in a hatchery. Scuba divers can monitor growth, health, and feeding by inspecting the fish daily.

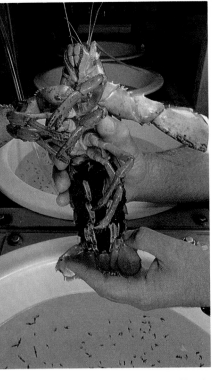

The New England Aquarium in Boston, Massachusetts, is one of a number of
public aquariums with an interest in animal life cycles and mariculture research.
Here a series of grow-out basins contain different stages in the development of the
northern lobster, *Homarus americanus*. The female lobster carries her eggs, or
"berries," tucked under her tail.

be beneficial in treating cancer and AIDS. Those that show promise
are cultured in large numbers for further study.[2]

Other researchers are experimenting with polyculture to see if
they can increase the yield of water-farming environments. Polyculture, first practiced centuries ago in Chinese fish ponds, is the cultivation of more than one species in the same water environment.
Scientists are trying to learn which species can coexist.

Hawaii is the site of a variety of maricultural research and
business enterprises. With its tropical climate, clear waters, seafood-
loving residents, and year-round growing season, Hawaii is proving to be an attractive sea-farming site. Since Hawaiians import 60
to 70 percent of the seafood they eat, government officials wish to
encourage the development of an island sea-farming industry.[3]

One company is farming different species of algae from which it
processes natural vitamin B and beta carotene for sale to drug
companies. (National Cancer Institute studies have suggested that
beta carotene may help reduce the risk of cancer.[4]) Another com-

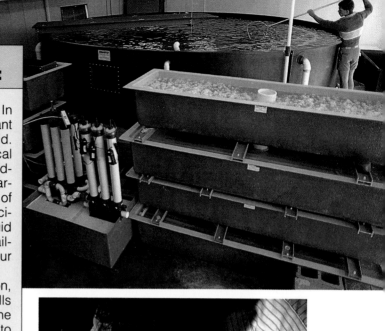

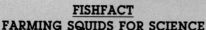
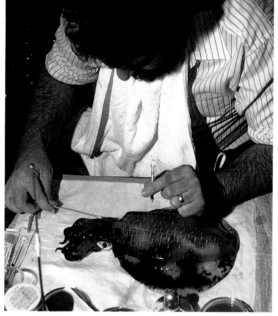

Scientists at the University of Texas Medical Branch at Galveston have become experts in the art of squid mariculture, in this case the Japanese oval squid, *Sepioteuthis lessoniana*. By cultivating squid in the laboratory, researchers have a ready supply of squid nervous systems to study for new knowledge about the human nervous system.

pany is experimenting with salmon, kelp, and oyster polyculture. Native to much colder waters, these species are thriving—not in the warm waters of coastal Hawaii but in icy nutrient-rich waters pumped up through pipes from depths of up to 2,000 feet (½ km) into onshore culturing tanks and ponds. This extraction of deep, cold water is part of the ocean thermal energy conversion (OTEC) project of the Natural Energy Lab of Hawaii. OTEC creates usable energy by utilizing the temperature difference between warm ocean water at the surface of the sea and cold seawater drawn up from great depths.

Today, we can only guess what the sea farm of the future will look like. Will it be onshore, offshore, or even far inland? Will it cover vast acres or relatively small space? Will its animals range freely or remain captive in tanks, ponds, or electronic corrals? One thing is certain, though. The sea farm of the future will surely use some brilliant technology. It will have to. As an industry, it is up against a vast array of environmental, political, and economic problems, many of which could one day be solved by technology.

THE ROLE OF AQUARIUMS IN MARICULTURE

As places where people can get close to living marine animals, aquariums from Boston to Bangkok provide pleasure and education for millions of visitors a year. Several aquariums, including ones in Monterey, California; Sydney, Australia; and Osaka, Japan; have made a specific commitment to aquaculture research.

Aquariums provide more than aquacultural research, though; they are an important avenue to learning about ocean resources. They also demonstrate how seriously the oceans are threatened today by human beings.

Part of the difficulty of establishing mariculture as an American industry lies in the distance people feel from the sea; many think of the oceans as endless, rather frightening bodies of water. Aquariums work hard to dispel these notions and prove that the world's oceans are places of wonder and beauty, of marvelous animals and plants, of new scientific knowledge, of frontiers waiting to be explored.

"Fish farming," says marine scientist John Ryther, "is not dependent upon nature. So, theoretically, there is really no upper limit to what it could produce.... But its future depends on the space and resources people are willing to give it."[5] Time will tell what space and resources mariculture will have. What seems abundantly clear is that without sea farming—and the science, technology, resource management, and financial commitments that go with it—we could face a future sadly empty of the bountiful fruits of the sea.

GLOSSARY

additives (ADD-uh-tivs): in the case of sea-weeds, these are sea-plant extracts that are added to other substances to improve their properties; algae extracts are added as thickeners in puddings, for example.

agronomy (Uh-GRON-uh-mee): the study of agricultural field-crop production.

anadromous fish (uh-NAD-ruh-mus): any species of fish that instinctively swims up-stream in fresh water to spawn; salmon are anadromous fish.

aquaculture (AK-wa-CUL-tcher): the prac-tice of cultivating plants and animals that live naturally in water; includes both freshwater and saltwater cultivation.

aquaculturist: one who practices aquacul-ture.

arthropods (AR-thruh-pods): invertebrates that have jointed bodies and limbs, and gen-erally an outer skeleton or shell; crustaceans, spiders, and insects are arthropods.

berried (BEH-reed): egg-bearing; the term refers to the thousands of berry-shaped eggs carried on the underside of a crustacean's body.

bivalve (BYE-valv): having a shell com-posed of two parts; also refers to an animal, such as an oyster, that has a two-part shell.

byssus (BISS-us): a tuft of long tough hairs by which some bivalves, such as mussels, attach themselves to a surface.

capture-fishing industry: refers to the catch-ing, trawling, or trapping of free-ranging sea animals that are to be sold.

crustaceans (crus-TAY-shuns): a large class of aquatic arthropods; lobsters, shrimp, and crabs are crustaceans.

cultch (KULCH): empty mollusk shells, usu-ally from oysters, that are laid down in oyster beds to serve as attachment surfaces for spat.

diatoms (DYE-uh-toms): tiny planktonic or bottom-dwelling algae.

ecology (ih-KOL-uh-gee): a branch of sci-ence concerned with the interrelationships among living things and their environments.

effluent (ef-FLEW-ent): something that flows out or is given off, such as waste material from a manufacturing plant.

fisheries: businesses involved with catching, packing, or selling fish or shellfish; also places for catching fish or taking sea animals.

freshwater aquaculture: the cultivation of plants and animals that naturally live in fresh water.

fry (FRYE): recently hatched fishes.

grow-out ponds: ponds made of earth or other materials in which aquatic animals are reared to adulthood.

habitats: the place where a plant or animal naturally or normally lives and grows.

husbandry: the cultivation or production of plants and animals; can also refer to the con-trol or use of resources.

hybrids (HYE-brids): offspring of two ani-mals or plants of different breeds, varieties, or species; a mule is the hybrid of a horse and a donkey.

integrated farming: the cultivation together of land-based plants and aquatic animals; an Asian farmer who rears milkfish in a rice paddy is practicing integrated farming.

kelp (KELP): large brown seaweeds with long, flat leaves supported in the water by round air bladders; when processed, used as an ingredient in various products, including toothpaste and salad oil.

mariculture (MAR-ih-cul-tcher): the cultiva-tion of plants and animals that live naturally in salt water.

market: the world of trade or economic ac-tivity; can refer to a set of public purchasing habits or preferences that determine what can be profitably bought and sold.

metric ton: equal to 2,240 pounds.

molt (MOWLT): to periodically shed, or cast off, an outer layer, such as a shell; crusta-ceans molt by casting off an existing shell, underneath which a new one is developing.

nacre (NA-ker): the iridescent inner layer of some mollusk shells.

nauplius (NAW-plee-us): a crustacean lar-va; generally the first form taken by the crus-tacean after the egg stage.

nori (NOE-ree): a bright purple, lobed sea-weed that is commercially farmed in Japan, China, and Taiwan; after processing, it is sold as a condiment and flavoring.

phytoplankton (fit-o-PLANK-ton): tiny aquatic plants that drift or float in large mass-es in a body of water.

postlarvae (post-LAR-vee): animals that have recently passed through the newly hatched stage; animals in the developmental stages that follow hatching.

quahog (KOE-hog): a thick-shelled American clam.

red seabream: a marine fish especially popular, and increasingly ranched and cage-farmed, in Japan.

saltwater aquaculture: the cultivation of plants and animals that naturally live in salt water; mariculture.

sea farm: any of a variety of locations where the cultivation of saltwater plants and animals takes place.

sea farming: the practice of cultivating saltwater plants and animals in which the farmer controls nearly every phase of the organism's life, from egg to harvest.

sea ranching: the practice of cultivating saltwater animals from eggs to juveniles and then releasing them to live in the ocean on their own; a common practice with anadromous fish, such as salmon and sturgeon, which return to their original hatcheries to spawn.

seaweeds: plants, such as any of the algae, that grow in salt water.

seed oysters: baby oysters, one to two inches (2½ to 5 cm) in size, that are generally hatchery-raised for sale to oyster farmers who cultivate them to maturity.

sluice: a passage for water, generally artificial, that is fitted with a gate or valve for stopping or regulating the flow of water.

smolt: a young salmon or sea trout, about two years old and five inches (13 cm) long, that is beginning to take on adult coloring.

spat (SPAT): a young oyster that settles on a hard surface to grow; before the life cycle of oysters was understood, people believed that oysters "spat out" their young.

spawn (SPAWN): to produce or deposit eggs, especially in large numbers; salmon and oysters spawn thousands of eggs at a time. Also used as a noun to refer to the eggs of aquatic animals; salmon eggs are called their spawn.

spore (SPOE-er): a seed produced by plants (and some invertebrates) that is capable of developing into a new individual after fusing with another spore.

stock enhancement: various actions that increase the numbers of certain animals, either domestic or wild; the ranching of salmon has contributed to salmon stock enhancement.

sushi: small cakes of cold rice wrapped in slices of raw fish and seaweed.

tidal flats: very shallow shoreline areas over which tides ebb and flow; oyster beds are commonly located in tidal flats.

trawling (TRAW-ling): the process, usually by boat, of dragging a large net over the sea bottom to gather fish and other marine life; wild-caught shrimp are gathered by trawling.

vertebrate (VER-teh-bret): an animal that has a backbone; refers to mammals, birds, reptiles, and fishes.

zoea (zo-EE-uh): an early larval form of many crustaceans, characterized by conspicuous eyes, large antennae, and mouth parts used for swimming.

zooplankton (ZO-eh-PLANK-ton): tiny aquatic animals that live in plankton masses.

SOURCE NOTES

CHAPTER 1: 1. Alexander McKee, *Farming the Sea* (New York: Thomas Y. Crowell, 1969) 32. **2.** E.S. Iverson, *Farming the Edge of the Sea* (Surrey: Fishing News Books, Ltd., 1976) 13. **3.** Jonathan Shepherd and Niall Bromage, *Intensive Fish Farming* (Cambridge: BSP Professional Books, 1988) 2. **4.** McKee, 35. **5.** John M. Kochiss, *Oystering From New York to Boston* (Middleton: Wesleyan University Press, 1974) 13. **6.** Phone interview with Dr. John Ryther, May 24, 1991. **7.** Phone interview with Population Division, United Nations, May 1991. **8.** *The Economist*, January 20, 1990, 14. **9.** Art Tiddens, *Aquaculture in America: The Role of Science, Government, and the Entrepreneur* (Boulder: Westview Press, 1990) 3. **10.** C.P. Idyll, *The Sea Against Hunger: Harvesting the Oceans to Feed a Hungry World* (New York: Thomas Y. Crowell, 1978) 90. **11.** U.S. Department of Agriculture, *Aquaculture Situation and Outlook Report:* March 1991, 5. **Sidebar: Mariculture and Agriculture 1.** Borgese, 73. **2.** ibid, 105. **3.** Kevin D. Hopkins and Emmanuel M. Cruz, The International Center for Living Aquatic Resources Management–Central Luzon State University Integrated Animal-Fish Farming Project: Final Report, 1982, 1-10.

CHAPTER 2: 1. U.S. Department of Agriculture, *Aquaculture Situation and Outlook Report:* March 1991, 16. **2.** John E. Bardach, John H. Ryther, and

William O. McLarney, *Aquaculture: The Farming and Husbandry of Freshwater and Marine Organisms* (New York: John Wiley & Sons, Inc., 1972) 588. **3.** "World Shrimp Farming 1990," *Aquaculture Digest*, January 1991. **4.** U.S.D.A. *Situation Report*, March 1991, 16. **5.** McKee, 124. **6.** Elisabeth Mann Borgese, *Seafarm* (New York: Harry N. Abrams, Inc., 1980) 163. **7.** *Sea Frontiers*, September/October 1983, 276. **8.** Bob Rosenberry, "World Shrimp Farming," *Aquaculture Magazine*, September/October 1990, 60. **9.** ibid, 61. **10.** Borgese, 143. **11.** Iverson, 142. **12.** Idyll, 72. **13.** Kochiss, 7. **14.** Idyll, 74; and Bardach et al., 688. **15.** Iverson, 150. **16.** Idyll, 72. **17.** Bardach et al., 716. **18.** Kochiss, 11. **19.** Phone interview with Dr. Hank Parker, director, Northeast Regional Aquaculture Center, North Dartmouth, Massachusetts, May 1991; and U.S.D.A. *Situation Report*, March 1991, 14. **20.** Phone interview with Dr. Hank Parker, May 1991; and *Seafood Leader*, March/April 1991, 173-4. **21.** *Seafood Leader*, September/October 1990, 115-16. **22.** "A Harvest of Numbers," 1990-91 Statistical Review, *Northern Aquaculture*, (Victoria, British Columbia), May/June 1991, 21. **23.** Borgese, 183. **24.** *World Aquaculture*, Vol. 19 (3), September, 1988, 54. **25.** Iverson, 123. **26.** E. Evan Brown, *World Fish Farming: Cultivation and Economics* (Westport: The Avi Publishing Company, 1977) 69; and interview with Dr. John Ryther, May 24, 1991. **27.** Bardach et al., 791. **28.** Borgese, 112. **29.** Iverson, 129. **30.** ibid, 125. **31.** Phone interview with Dr. Ryther, May 24, 1991. **32.** Borgese, 115-120. **Sidebar: Developing a Good Set of Mussels 1.** Borgese, 131. **2.** Iverson, 166. **3.** ibid, 158-167. **4.** Borgese, 131. **5.** Koch, 43.

CHAPTER 3: 1. Idyll, 65. **2.** Bardach, 186-88. **3.** McKee, 41. **4.** Idyll, 76. **5.** Iverson, 61; and Jonathan Bartlett, *The Ocean Environment* (New York: H.W. Wilson, 1977), 27. **6.** ibid Bartlett, 27. **7.** Iverson, 181. **8.** McKee, 124. **9.** Shepherd and Bromage, 73-74. **10.** *Sea Frontiers*, September/October 1990, 42. **11.** Phone interview with Peter Moore, executive director, Maine Aquaculture Innovation Center, Orono, Maine, May 1991. **12.** Borgese, 195.

CHAPTER 4: 1. Phone interview with Scott Lindell, AquaFuture, Inc., Montague, Massachusetts, May 1991. **2.** Koch, Frances King, "Farming the Fruits of the Sea," *Aquasphere Magazine, Journal of the New England Aquarium*, Boston, Massachusetts, Winter 1990-91, 43. **3.** Idyll, 203.

CHAPTER 5: 1. Iverson, 114-117. **2.** Phone interview with Dr. Kenneth M. Snader, Natural Products Branch, National Cancer Institute, Bethesda, Maryland, June 17, 1991. **3.** Phone interview with John Corbin, manager, Aquaculture Development Program, Department of Land and Natural Resources, University of Hawaii, Honolulu, Hawaii, June 21, 1991. **4.** Diana Lomont, "Keahole Point—Where Salty Profits Are In the Works," *Hawaii Investor*, May 1990, 13-20. **5.** Phone interview with Dr. Ryther, May 24, 1991.

FOR FURTHER READING

Aquaculture Digest, January 1991

Aquaculture Magazine, September/October 1990

Bardach, John. *Harvest of the Sea*. New York: Harper & Row, 1968

Bardach, John, and John H. Ryther and William O. McLarney. *Aquaculture: The Farming and Husbandry of Freshwater and Marine Organisms*. New York: John Wiley & Sons, Inc., 1972

Barnet, Richard J. *The Lean Years, Politics in the Age of Scarcity*. New York: Simon and Schuster, 1980

Bartlett, Jonathan. *The Ocean Environment*. New York: Thomas Y. Crowell, 1969

Bayer, Robert and Juanita. *Lobsters Inside-out, A Guide to the Maine Lobster*. Bar Harbor: Acadia Press, 1989

Borgese, Elisabeth Mann. *Seafarm*. New York: Harry N. Abrams, Inc., 1980

Brown, E. Evan. *World Fish Farming: Cultivation and Economics*. Westport: The Avi Publishing Company, 1977

Butler, Michael J.A. "Plight of the Bluefin Tuna." *National Geographic Magazine*, August 1982.

Cousteau, Jacques. *The Living Sea*. New York: Harper & Row, 1963

Fralick, Richard A. and John H. Ryther. "Uses and Cultivation of Seaweeds." *Oceanus Magazine*, Summer 1976 (Woods Hole Oceanographic Institute)

Hass, Hans. *Beneath the Sea, Man's Conquest of the Underwater World*. New York: St. Martin's Press, 1973

Idyll, C.P. *The Sea Against Hunger, Harvesting the Oceans to Feed a Hungry World*. New York: Thomas Y. Crowell, 1978

Iverson, E.S. *Farming the Edge of the Sea*. Surrey: Fishing News Books, Ltd., 1976

Jasperson, William. *A Day in the Life of a Marine Biologist*. New York: Little, Brown, 1982

Kochiss, John M. *Oystering from New York to Boston*. Middleton: Wesleyan University Press, 1974

Mann, Roger. "Exotic Species in Aquaculture." *Oceanus Magazine*, Spring 1979.

Marx, Wesley. *The Oceans: Our Last Resource*. San Francisco: Sierra Club Books, 1981

McKee, Alexander. *Farming the Sea*. New York: Thomas Y. Crowell, 1969

Ormond, Rupert. *The Living Ocean.* Chicago: Children's Press, 1982

Russell, Sir Frederick. *The Seas, An Introduction to the Study of Life in the Sea.* London: Frederick Warne & Co., Ltd., 1975

Ryther, John H. "Aquaculture in China." *Oceanus Magazine*, Spring 1979. Woods Hole Oceanographic Institute

————. "Mariculture: How Much Protein and For Whom?" *Oceanus Magazine*, Winter 1975.

Schwind, Phil. *Practical Shellfish Farming.* Camden: International Marine Publishing Company, 1977

Sea Frontiers Magazine, September/October 1983.

Seafood Leader Magazine, March/April 1991.

Shepherd, Jonathan and Niall Bromage. *Intensive Fish Farming.* Cambridge: BSP Professional Books, 1988

Taylor, Herb. *The Lobster: Its Life Cycle.* New York: Pisces Books, 1984

Tiddens, Art. *Aquaculture in America, The Role of Science, Government, and the Entrepreneur.* Boulder: Westview Press, Inc., 1990

U.S. Department of Commerce, National Oceanic and Atmospheric Administration. *Fisheries of the United States, 1989.* U.S.D.A./N.O.A.A., Washington D.C., May 1990

Van Dyk, Jere. "Long Journey of the Pacific Salmon." *National Geographic Magazine*, July 1990.

INDEX

Algae farming, 50–51
American mariculture, 5, 9–11, 21, 28, 31, 33, 35, 36, 37, 40, 43, 49, 52
Aquaculture. *See* Mariculture
Aquariums and mariculture, 52

Bardach, John, 36
Bay scallop farming, 28
Beta carotene, 50
British mariculture, 8–9, 28

Cage culture, 43
California, 31
Canadian mariculture, 28, 43
Chinese mariculture, 21, 31, 33, 50
Christmas Carol, A, 25
Clam farming, 28
Crossbreeding, 49

Depletion of ocean animals, 9, 10–11, 52
Dickens, Charles, 25
Dutch mariculture, 28

Economic problems, mariculture's, 45–46, 52
Ecuadoran mariculture, 21, 23
Environmental problems, mariculture's, 46, 52
Eucheuma farming, 33

Finfish farming, 18, 28–31, 35, 40–41, 43, 51
Fishing, traditional, 11, 14
Florida, 28
Food production and mariculture, 5, 11–14
French mariculture, 27, 28, 36
Freshwater aquaculture, 8

Garfield, Seth, 37
Genetic manipulation, 49
Grow-out farming, 36

Harvest of the Sea, 36
Hatchery farming, 36
Hawaiian mariculture, 21, 31, 50

Idyll, C. P., 11, 47
Indonesian mariculture, 8, 35
Invertebrates, 17

Japanese mariculture, 8, 19, 27, 28, 31–33, 42, 46

Kelp farming, 51

Laminaria farming, 33
Lantern nets, 5, 37
Legal problems, mariculture's, 45
Lobster farming, 19

Maine, 33
Mariculture:
    challenges of, 45–47
    history of, 7–11
    methods of sea farming, 35–43
    need for increased food production, 11–14
    science of, 49–52
    species suited to sea farming, 17–33
Massachusetts, 5, 37
Mexican mariculture, 21
Milkfish farming, 40–41
Mollusks, 23–25
Mussel farming, 40

National Cancer Institute, 49, 50
National Energy Lab, 51
Nori farming, 31–33
Norwegian mariculture, 31, 35, 43

Ocean farming. *See* Mariculture
Ocean thermal energy conversion (OTEC), 51
Orata, Sergius, 8
Oyster farming, 5, 8–9, 18, 25–28, 35, 36, 40, 51

Philippine mariculture, 27, 33, 42
Phytoplankton, 27
Pollution and mariculture, 10, 11, 46, 49
Polyculture, 50–51
Pond culture, 5, 40–42
Protection and restocking of ocean animals, 5
Puerto Rico, 21

Raft-and-line culture, 36, 40
Red seabream, 31
Roman mariculture, 8
Ryther, John, 47, 52

Salmon farming, 18, 28–31, 35, 43, 51
Scientific research and mariculture, 5, 45, 49–52

Scotch mariculture, 43
Sea Against Hunger, The, 11
Sea ranching, 35–36
Seaweed farming, 18, 31–33
Shrimp farming, 18, 19–23, 35, 41, 42
South Carolina, 21, 28
Spanish mariculture, 40
Squid farming, 49
Study projects, 33, 43, 47
Sturgeon, 31

Taiwan mariculture, 33
Tank culture, 40, 42
Texas, 21, 49
Trawling for shrimp, 19

Undaria farming, 33
United Nations Food and Agricultural Organization, 47

Virginia, 28
Vitamin B, 50

Woods Hole Oceanographic Institute, 47
World food supply and mariculture, 11, 45, 47, 52

Yellowtail, 31

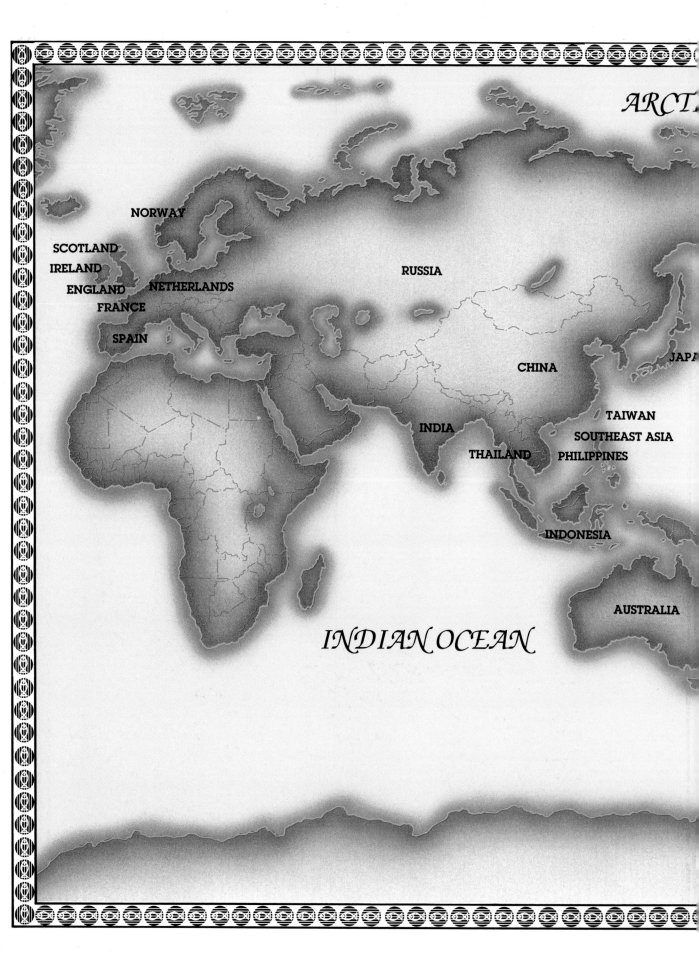